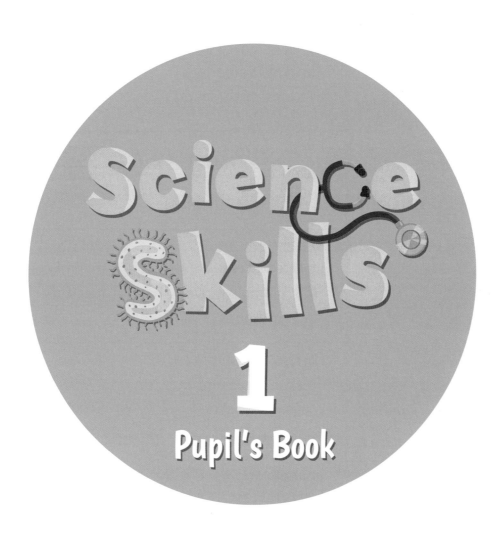

Science Skills

1

Pupil's Book

by

Estrella Alarcón   Cristina Domínguez   Berta Quesada

CAMBRIDGE
UNIVERSITY PRESS

SCIENCE SKILLS 1

Contents

· Introduction to the course characters

· Bones, joints and muscles
· Parts of the body
· Sections of the body
· Parts of the face
· Senses

· Food groups
· Five a day
· Sport
· Healthy habits

· Vertebrates and invertebrates
· How animals move
· Animal groups
· Wild and domestic animals
· Habitats

· Parts of a plant
· Trees, bushes and grasses
· Wild and cultivated plants
· What plants make

· The circle of life: plants, animals and people are living things
· What living things need
· Non-living things

· Good and bad choices
· Behaviour at school and at home
· Helping at home

Projects and experiments	Mindful time	Documentaries
· Build a skeleton. · Make a Body mini book. · Make a potion.	· Belly breathing	· Incredible bodies
· Keep a food diary. · Find out why we need to brush our teeth.	· Contract and relax your body parts	· In the supermarket
· Make an animal habitat. · Find out what birds eat.	· Sounds of nature	· Animal trip
· Find out what plants need to live.	· Breathe like a tree	· All about plants
· Make a crazy garden. · Make an animal poster. · The time of my life!	· Sensations	· Living and non-living things
· Make a postbox for positive messages. · Do a survey to find out what chores your classmates do.	· Mirrors	· Good choices

Story 1 → Page 90   Story 2 → Page 92   Story 3 → Page 94

MEET OUR SCIENTISTS

I like studying the human body.

Little Franklin

I like healthy food and I love milk!

Little Pasteur

I love animals.

Little Cuvier

I know a lot about plants.

Little Aristotle

I am interested in living things.

Little Linnaeus

Thanks to me, doctors can use X-rays.

Little Curie

I can think, predict, experiment, observe and conclude. **I am a scientist too**!

Scientific method:
1 Predict
2 Experiment
3 Observe and conclude

Scientist card

Print your finger here when you complete a unit.

Name:

Age:

Welcome Unit	Unit 1	Unit 2	Unit 3	Unit 4	Unit 5	Unit 6

What do you like? Circle.

bones and skeletons

plants

healthy food

family

sport

friends

DOCUMENTARY
Incredible bodies

ARE BONES HARD OR SOFT?

Find out

Point to your joints. Practise saying them.

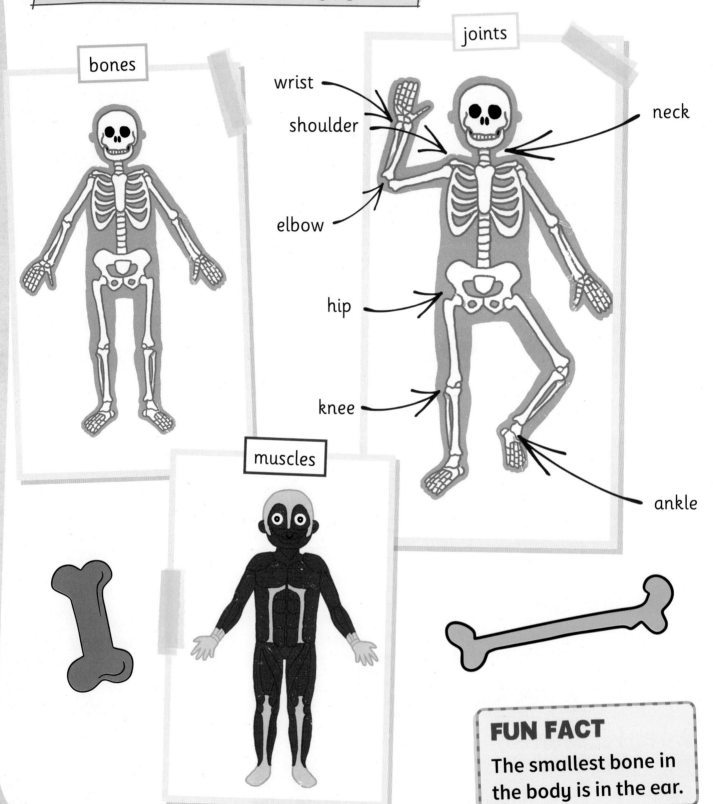

bones

joints

wrist

shoulder

neck

elbow

hip

knee

ankle

muscles

FUN FACT

The smallest bone in the body is in the ear.

Mini-project

? What's in the box?

1 Bones! Build a skeleton. Connect the bones.

2 The skeleton needs joints. Work together.

What have I learnt?

Bones are hard.

Joints and muscles help us move.

My ankle and my knees are joints.

MY DICTIONARY

ankle

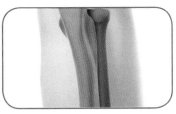

bones

joints

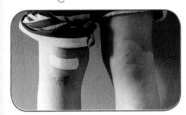

knees

muscles

HOW MANY LIMBS HAVE YOU GOT?

Find out

Point to the limbs.

arm

fingers

tummy

bottom

leg

foot

toes

head

torso

limbs

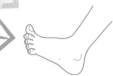

FUN FACT

Pau Gasol, from arm to arm, is wider than he is tall.

Mini-project

Let's make a Body mini book.

1 Write your name and stick your photo on the cover!

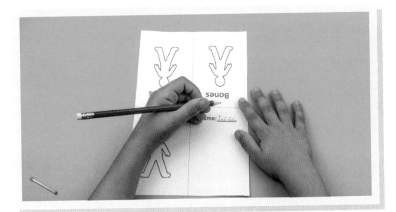

2 Colour your muscles, your bones and your joints. Use a different colour for each.

Fold the page to make your mini book.

What have I learnt?

My body has got three sections:
a head, torso and limbs.
Arms and legs are limbs.

MY DICTIONARY

arms

head

legs

limbs

torso

11

ARE ALL EYES BLUE?

Find out

Draw the missing lines.

1 eyes

2 eyelashes

3 eyebrows

4 ears

5 cheeks

6 nose

7 mouth

8 tongue

9 chin

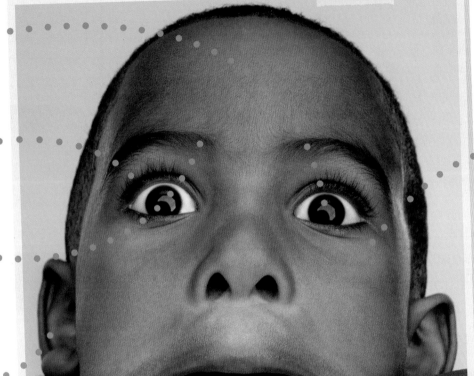

FUN FACT
Your ears and nose continue growing all your life!

Find an animal's nose hidden in the unit!

Game Zone

Try it out

🎧 Listen and draw your monster.

MY DICTIONARY

ears

eyes

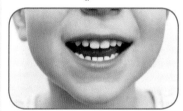

mouth

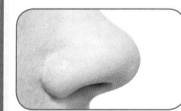

nose

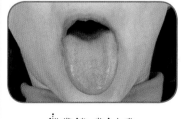

tongue

What have I learnt?

I have got two ears, two eyes, one mouth, one nose and one tongue.

CAN YOU SEE IN THE DARK?

Trace the words. Practise saying them.

see

taste

hear

touch

smell

FUN FACT

This picture is magic.
What can you see?

Experiment

Make a potion. Use your senses.

1 Cover your eyes and smell each ingredient.

I think this is …

SOAP

VINEGAR

2 Mix three of the things together. Then, smell the potion.

SOAP

VINEGAR

Conclusion
How does it smell?

15

1 Do yoga with your teacher. Which body parts are you using?

2 Mindful practice. Eat using your five senses.

1 Cover your eyes. **2** Touch your food. **3** Smell your food.

4 Listen to your food. **5** Open your eyes. **6** Taste your food!

Now I know

Assessment link
Go to page 78 for more activities.

1 🎧 Listen and number the body parts.

2 Draw a line from the organ to the sense.

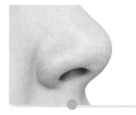   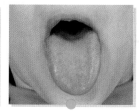 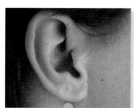

| smell | taste | see | hear | touch |

Chant
Five senses

I am Rosalind Franklin.
I studied the human body.

17

2

STAY STRONG, LIVE LONG!

Can you see any food?

What is your favourite snack?

Mindful

Contract and relax your body parts.

time

S♪ng
I like healthy food!

I always bring healthy snacks to school. I like fruit, carrots and sandwiches.

D▶CUMENTARY
In the supermarket

19

ARE ALL VEGETABLES GREEN?

Circle your favourite food in each group.

Find out

carbohydrates

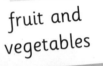

fruit and vegetables

proteins

dairy

Yogurt

low fat milk

fats

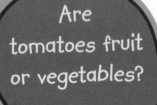

Are tomatoes fruit or vegetables?

FUN FACT

Strawberries are the only fruit that have their seeds on the outside.

Pr⚙ject Step 1

Try it out

? What's in the box?

1 Food! Classify it into groups.

2 Make a food diary. Draw what you had for breakfast this morning. Which food groups does it belong to?

What have I learnt?

There are five food groups:
1 dairy
2 fats
3 fruit and vegetables
4 carbohydrates
5 proteins

MY DICTIONARY

dairy

fats

fruit and vegetables

carbohydrates

proteins

WHY IS WATER GOOD FOR YOU?

Find out

Draw another healthy snack.

healthy snacks

unhealthy snacks

Tip
Eat five times a day and don't forget to drink water!

breakfast

snack

lunch

snack

dinner

FUN FACT

10 sugar cubes = 1 can of cola

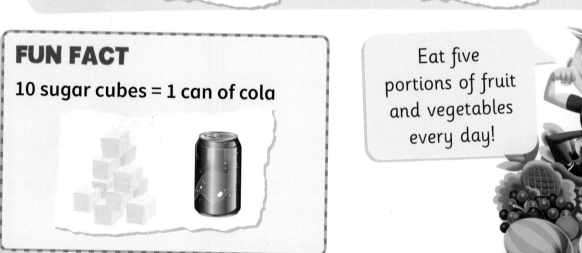

Eat five portions of fruit and vegetables every day!

Pr⚙️je✂️ct Step 2

Add more information to your food diary.

1 Add your snack, lunch and dinner to your diary. Draw.

2 Tell your partner.

3 Circle the healthy food in your diary.

What have I learnt?

It is very healthy to eat five times a day:

1 breakfast   4 snack

2 snack   5 dinner

3 lunch

Try it out

MY DICTIONARY

breakfast

snack

lunch

dinner

How much food in your diary is healthy?

IS WALKING GOOD FOR YOU?

Find out

Tell a classmate your favourite sport.

Sport keeps you **fit** and **healthy**.
Your **heart** and **muscles** grow strong.

3 Golden Rules

1 **30 minutes** of sport every day.

2 **Sleep 10 hours** a day.

3 **1 hour** of TV or video games a day, only.

Find the basketball hidden in the unit!

SUPER-HUMAN FACT

The world record for the 100 metre sprint is 9.58 seconds!

Game Zone

1 Play *Steal the ball.*

1 Get into two groups and line up.
Give everyone in each group a number.

2 The teacher places a ball between the teams and calls a number.

3 The first player to take the ball to their team without being tagged is the winner!

2 How do you feel after playing? Tick (✓).

☐ happy   ☐ calm   ☐ angry   ☐ sad

MY DICTIONARY

keep fit

sport

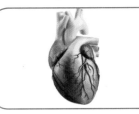

heart

muscles

What have I learnt?

Sport is good for my heart and muscles.
It helps me keep fit.

Find out

Brush your teeth after you eat.

Wash your hands.

Have a shower every day.

SOAP

Who is doing the right thing? Tick (✓).

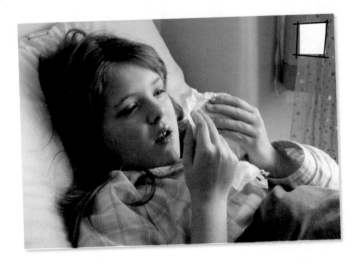

26

Experiment

Find out what cola, vinegar and water do to eggs.

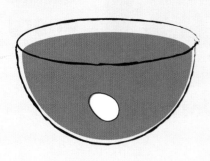  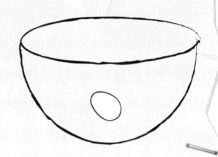

1 Put an egg in cola. Observe it for **a day**.

2 Put another egg in **vinegar**. Observe it for **two days**.

3 Put a third egg in **water**. Observe it for **three days**.

What happens to egg number 1?

What happens to egg number 2?

What happens to egg number 3?

Conclusion

Which egg changed first?

Which egg stayed healthy?

What happens if you do not brush your teeth?

1 When do you feel ...?

happy

calm

sad

worried

angry

2 🎧 How does Lucy feel? Listen and tick (✓).

3 How do you feel today? Draw and colour.

Now I know

Assessment link
Go to page 80 for more activities.

1 Draw one more item in each section of the food wheel. Colour.

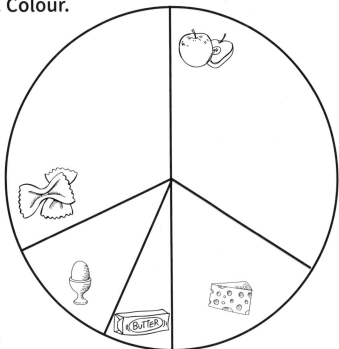

2 Circle the healthy habits.

3 Look at the pictures. Look at the letters. Write the words.

_ _ _ _ _   r u i f t   _ _ _ _ _   t s p o r

Chant
Be healthy

I am Louis Pasteur.
I developed the first vaccinations, to stop people from getting sick.

29

Song
Move like an animal

Who is sad? Why are they sad?

DOCUMENTARY
Animal trip

ARE ALL FISH THE SAME?

Draw a vertebrate in the box.

A jellyfish is an **invertebrate**.

A balloon fish is a **vertebrate**.

no skeleton

skeleton

Why is it called a *jellyfish*?

Why is it called a *balloon fish*?

Find the hidden octopus in the unit!

FUN FACT

An electric eel can make electricity for ten light bulbs!

Pr🔧ject Step 1

Let's explore the ocean!

1 Find a shoe box. Draw an ocean background.

2 Draw, colour and stick the animals in the ocean.

Point to the vertebrates and invertebrates.

MY DICTIONARY

balloon fish

crab

invertebrate

vertebrate

What have I learnt?

A vertebrate has got a skeleton.
An invertebrate has not got a skeleton.
A crab is an invertebrate.
A balloon fish is a vertebrate.

CAN POLAR BEARS SWIM?

Find out

Colour the jumping fish.

walk

fly

slither

FUN FACT

A polar bear's fur is transparent!

Why do you think it looks white?

swim

Project **Step 2**

Now let's go to the Arctic!

1 Find a shoe box. Draw an Arctic background.

2 Draw, colour and stick the animals to the Arctic.

Say how the animals move!

Try it out

MY DICTIONARY

fly

slither

swim

walk

What have I learnt?

Animals move in different ways.
They can slither, walk, fly and swim.

IS A BAT A BIRD?

Find and circle the stick insect.

Find out

mammal

bird

reptile

amphibian

fish

FUN FACT

A baby koala is the size of a gummy bear!

Did you find the stick insect? Why do you think it is called a stick insect?

Project Step 3

Let's finish our adventure in the rainforest.

1 Find a shoe box. Draw a forest background.

2 Draw, colour and stick the animals to the forest.

Say how the animals move!

What have I learnt?

There are five types of vertebrate:

amphibians   mammals
birds   reptiles
fish

Display your adventures in your classroom!

MY DICTIONARY

amphibians

birds

fish

mammals

reptiles

ARE ALL ANIMALS GOOD PETS?

🎧 Listen and circle the correct animal.

wild

domestic

FUN FACT
Chicks lose their feathers when they are worried!

Experiment

Find out what birds eat.

1 Cut some windows in a milk carton. Make two holes near the bottom and put a stick through them.

2 Fill the carton with different food: breadcrumbs, corn, cereal and seeds.

3 Hang the carton outside and observe.

predict

Which food do you think the birds will like the most?

You can also paint and decorate your milk carton.

Conclusion

What is the birds' favourite food?

breadcrumbs   corn   cereal   seeds

Was your prediction correct?

1 Do animal yoga with your teacher. Which animal is your favourite?

dog

snake

cat

cow

monkey

butterfly

2 Look after pets. Match the sentences to the correct picture.

Feed your pet.

Wash your pet.

Play with your pet.

Never abandon your pet!

Assessment link
Go to page 82 for more activities.

1 🎧 Listen and circle the invertebrates.

a

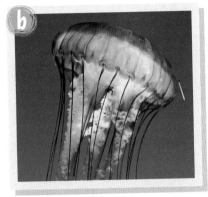
b

c

d

e

f

2 Can you remember? Classify the animals.

cat   fox   hen   badger   tiger   horse

domestic animals	wild animals

Chant
Wild, domestic

I am George Cuvier.
I studied animals all over the world.

41

Song
I am a plant

What do plants need to live?

How does Little Curie feel?

DOCUMENTARY
All about plants

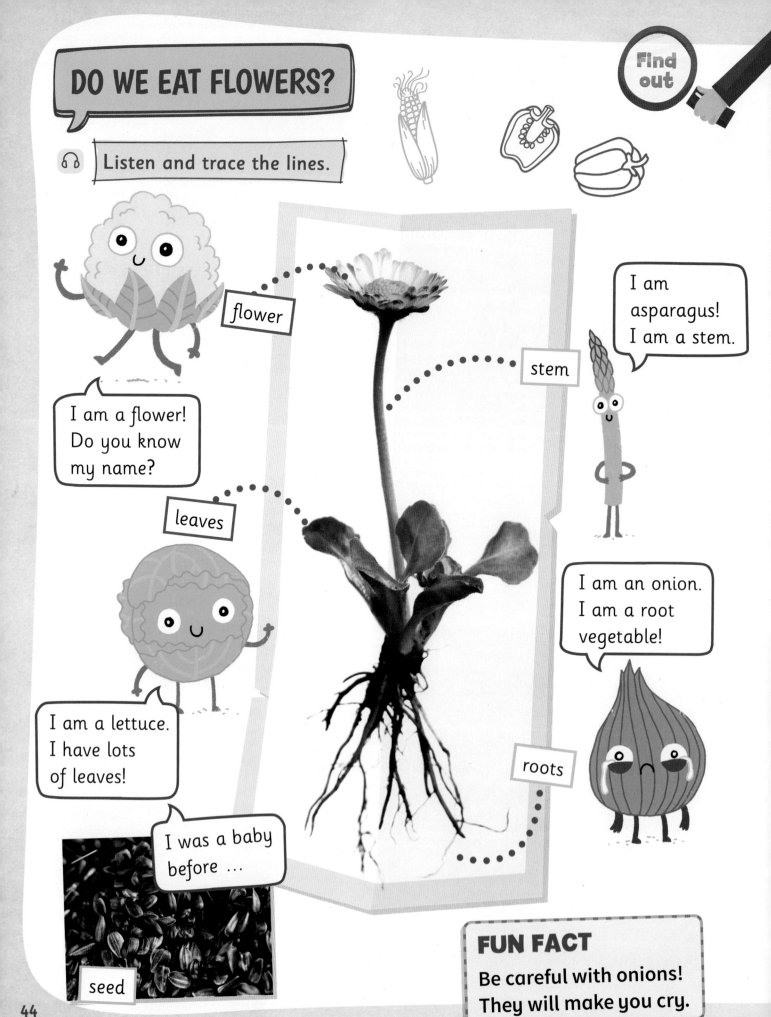

DO WE EAT FLOWERS?

🎧 Listen and trace the lines.

flower

stem

I am asparagus! I am a stem.

I am a flower! Do you know my name?

leaves

I am an onion. I am a root vegetable!

I am a lettuce. I have lots of leaves!

I was a baby before …

roots

seed

FUN FACT

Be careful with onions! They will make you cry.

Project Step 1

? What's in the box?

1 Seeds! Let's germinate them!
Wet a cloth with water. Put some seeds in the cloth. Place the cloth in a bag and seal it.

2 Everyone in the class hangs their bag next to a window.

Predict

What do you think will happen?

MY DICTIONARY

flowers

leaves

roots

seeds

stem

What have I learnt?

Plants have got f_____ ,
l_____ , r_____ and
a s_____ .
Some plants grow from s_____ .

45

IS GRASS ALWAYS GREEN?

Find out

What food can you see?

Some trees and bushes give us fruit!

tree

branch

thick trunk

bush

woody stems

grass

Grass is bendy.

Wheat is grass too!

FUN FACT

Plants cry for help when they are thirsty, but no one can hear them!

Pr🔗ject Step 2

What do plants drink?

1 Work in groups. Take three plants from the line. Add cola to one of the plants. Add vinegar to another one.

2 Add water to the third. Let's call this plant *Control plant* – write it on the bag.

predict

What will happen to the plants?

Control plant

Hang the bags up again. Make sure they are closed.

What have I learnt?

Trees have got a t_____ .
Bushes have got lots of w_____
s_____ .
G_____ is bendy.

MY DICTIONARY

bush

grass

tree

trunk

woody stems

DO ALL PLANTS NEED US TO LOOK AFTER THEM?

Find out

What other wild plants do you know?

strawberry field

pine tree field

cotton field

chamomile field

thistles

We are **wild**!

What else do farmers work with?

farmer

cultivated

algae

dandelions

FUN FACT

Wild plants grow everywhere! From the tops of mountains to the deep ocean.

Project Step 3

Do plants need sunlight?

1 Work in your groups. Take a new bag from the line. Put it in a drawer.

2 Observe the new plant and the *Control plant*. What happens to each plant?

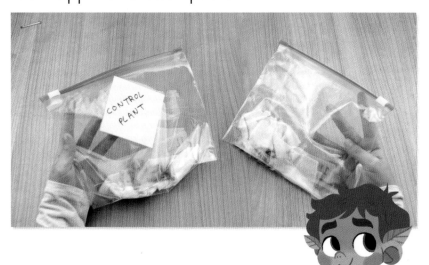

CONTROL PLANT

MY DICTIONARY

cotton

cultivated

farmer

fields

wild

What have I learnt?

W_____ plants grow everywhere.
A farmer grows c_____ plants
in f_____ .
C_____ is a cultivated plant.

49

WHERE DOES PAPER COME FROM?

Find out

Plants are helpful! Point to the things you use every day.

strawberry jam

strawberries

food

pine trees

tables and chairs

furniture

cotton

t-shirts

clothes

chamomile

chamomile tea

medicine

Find the sunflower hidden in the unit!

Pr⚙ject Step 4

What do plants need? Circle the correct face.

①   water

     cola or vinegar

Plants need w_____ .

②   cupboard

     window

Plants need s_____light.

Plants also need **air**.

Take your *Control plant* out of the bag and put it in soil, inside a plastic container. You will need it for the next unit!

MY DICTIONARY

clothes

food

furniture

medicine

What have I learnt?

We use plants to make c_____ ,
fu_____ , m_____ ,
and f_____ .

1 How do we take care of plants? Tick (✓) the correct behaviour.

a Water plants.

b Let plants have sunlight and fresh air.

c Put plants in a cupboard.

d Pick wild flowers and plants.

e Step on plants.

2 How do you feel when you breathe like a tree?
Circle the word and draw a face.

a sad

b happy

c calm

d worried

Now I know

✓ **Assessment link**
Go to page 84 for more activities.

1 🎧 Listen and draw lines to the pictures.

cultivated ●

wild ●

●  ●  ●  ●  ●

2 Draw a plant and label the parts.

roots   leaves   stem   flower

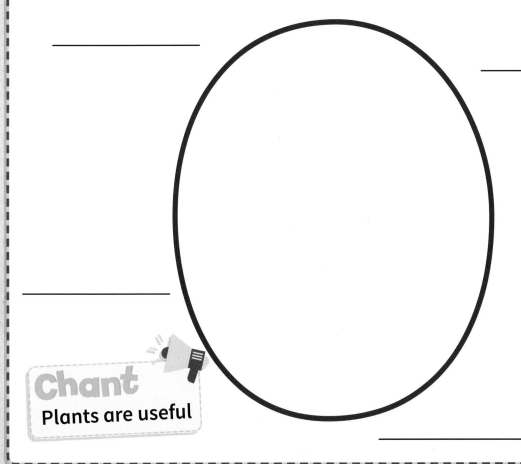

_____

_____

_____

_____

Chant
Plants are useful

I am Aristotle.
I studied and classified plants.

I'M ALIVE!

What food can you see?

Mindful

Sensations

time

Song
I'm alive

Are coconuts living things?

What is Little Linnaeus doing?

What is Little Pasteur doing?

DOCUMENTARY
Living and non-living things

55

DO PLANTS LIVE FOREVER?

Colour the sunflower.

Plants

1 Plants are born.

2 Plants grow.

Plants are living things

4 Plants die.

3 Plants reproduce.

What do plants need?

FOOD

WATER

AIR

FUN FACT

Plants use sunlight to make their own food.

56

Project Step 1

Let's make a crazy garden!

1 More plants! Take the *Control plant* from Unit four.

2 In the same plastic container, plant a plastic flower next to the *Control plant*.

Observe!
What do you
think will happen?

MY DICTIONARY

born

grow

reproduce

die

What have I learnt?

Plants are _____ , they _____ ,
_____ and _____ .
Plants are living things.

DO ANIMALS HAVE FAMILIES?

How many baby animals can you see? Circle.

Find out

Animals

Animals die.

Animals are living things.

Animals reproduce.

Animals grow.

What do animals need?

Animals are born.

○
○
○

FOOD   WATER   AIR

I want a salad!

FUN FACT

Gorillas are herbivores, they don't eat meat.

Find the kitten hidden in the unit!

Mini-project

Try it out

? | **What's in the box?**

1 Animals! Let's make an animal poster.

2 Draw the things animals need. Make a poster and show it to other groups!

Do animals need the same things as plants?

living things

food

water

air

What have I learnt?

Animals need _____ , _____
and _____ .
Animals are _____ .

59

DO WE CHANGE AS WE GROW?

Find out

Circle the oldest person on the page.

People

People are living things!

1 People are born.

baby

2 People grow.

boy

girl

3 People reproduce and get old.

FUN FACT

A baby is born in the world every three seconds.

What do you need to live?

FOOD

WATER

AIR

Mini-project

The time of my life!

1 Make a table for the different stages of your life.

2 Add your photos. Draw yourself in the future.
Do you look the same?

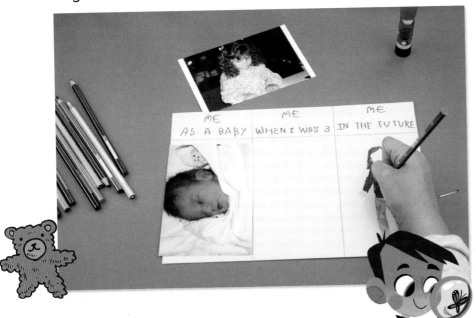

MY DICTIONARY

baby

boy

girl

adult

What have I learnt?

When you are born, you are a _____ .
You grow into a _____ or a _____ .
You keep growing and become an _____ .

Draw your favourite toy now and in the future! Is it different?

DO ALL THINGS GROW?

What non-living things can you see in your classroom?

The sun, clouds and rocks are non-living things.

clouds

sun

rocks

A chair, a sand castle and a ball are non-living things.

Project Step 2

Circle the correct answer.

Let's look at the crazy garden!

MY DICTIONARY

non-living things

chairs

clouds

rocks

		Yes	No
1 Are the plants in the container different?		Yes	No
2 Does the plastic flower grow?		Yes	No
3 Does the *Control plant* grow?		Yes	No

Which one is a living thing? Why?

What have I learnt?

There are many _____-_____ things.
Chairs, _____ and _____
are non-living things.

Attitude is everything

1 **Let's make a *calm down bottle*!**

1 Get your materials ready.

2 Put glue in the bottle and paint.

3 Add glitter and beads.

4 Add water.

5 Put the top on.

6 Shake it!

… and breathe!

2 **Use the *calm down bottle* to feel calm when …**

you are angry.

you are sad.

the classroom is noisy.

Now I know

Assessment link

Go to page 86 for more activities.

1 Classify the following things.

tree

rock

window

person

fish

sand

living things	non-living things

2 🎧 Listen and draw a living and non-living thing.

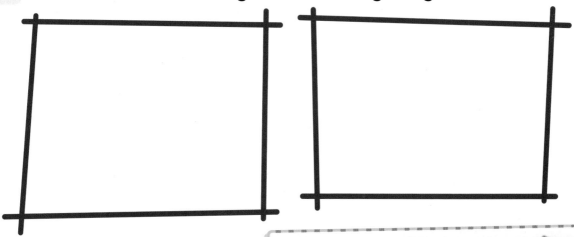

Chant

Is it living?

I am Carl Linnaeus.

I was a scientist and I gave names to groups of living things.

ARE YOU A GREAT PERSON?

Find out

Write your name on the star. Colour it.

I can share.

I am nice.

I can give my opinion.

I am clever.

I can help.

I am kind.

We can all be great!

Project Step 1

Let's make a postbox.

1 Make and decorate your postbox.

2 Write a nice message for yourself and post it!

I am kind.   I can share.

MY DICTIONARY

clever

help

kind

nice

share

What have I learnt?

I am _____ , _____
and _____ .
I can _____ and _____ .

69

ARE YOU A GOOD FRIEND?

Find out

🎧 Listen and point.

Play fair.

Don't be a bully.

Take care of little ones.

Different, but best friends.

I am sorry

Be honest.

Pr😊ject Step 2

Write a message for your friend.

1 In your class, put all of your names in a bowl.

2 Take a name and write a positive message for that person.

3 Turn the paper over and draw your friend as a superhero.

You are kind to others.

You are honest.

Try it out

What have I learnt?

To be a good friend:
play _____ , don't be a _____ ,
take _____ of little ones
and be _____ .

Put the message in your friend's postbox!

ARE YOU A GOOD CLASSMATE?

Point to the super classmates in the picture.

When do you say *please*?   Do you like working together?

Train your brain by working hard!

ALWAYS TRY TO ...

- work hard.
- try your best.
- help each other.
- take care of classroom materials.

SAY ...

- please
- thank you
- well done!
- Can I help you?

Project Step 3

Let's write a message for the class.

1 Write a positive message for the whole class.

2 Share your messages with your classmates!

We help each other.

MY DICTIONARY

help each other

say well done

try your best

work hard

What have I learnt?

Super classmates _____ hard, _____
their best and _____ each other.
Super classmates say _____ _____ .

73

DO YOU HELP AT HOME?

Draw another thing you do at home.

What do you do at home?

Get my schoolbag ready.

Make my bed.

Respect my family.

Keep calm.

Listen to others.

Tidy up my room.

Tidy up your room and find your treasures.

Find the schoolbag hidden in the unit!

Mini-project

Work in groups and complete the table.
Colour the boxes to show what you do at home.

Name	I make my bed.	I get my schoolbag ready.	I respect my family.	I keep calm.

get my schoolbag ready

keep calm

make my bed

respect my family

Do you keep calm?

Yes, I do. / No, I don't.

What have I learnt?

In the morning, I _____ my bed
and _____ my schoolbag ready.
I _____ my family and
keep _____ .

1 **Make your star.**

1 Choose one of the messages from your postbox.

2 Glue it to your star.

We are all stars!

3 Colour and cut out your star.

4 Hang it up in the classroom.

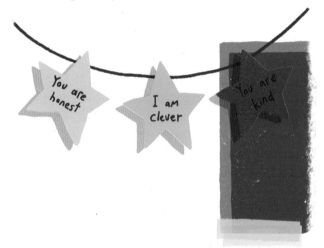

2 **How do you feel when you read your messages? Tick (✓).**

Why do you feel like this?

Assessment link
Go to page 88 for more activities.

1 Tick (✓) the good choices.

ⓐ

I don't play fair.

ⓑ

I'm not a bully.

ⓒ

I work hard.

ⓓ

I make my bed.

ⓔ

I help others.

2 🎧 Listen and complete the good behaviours list.

- I r_____ my family.
- I l_____ to others.
- I am n_____ .
- I make my b_____ .
- I t_____ my room.

YOU ARE A SUPER CLASSMATE!

Chant
I am a star

I am Marie Curie.
Thanks to me, doctors can use x-rays!

77

Find the right words

1 🎧 Listen and circle the correct words.

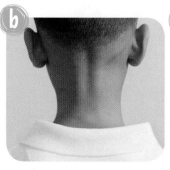
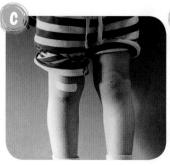

This is / These are my tongue.

This is / These are my neck.

This is / These are my knees.

This is / These are my elbows.

2 Choose the correct questions. Ask and answer with a partner.

a What's this? / What are these?   They are eyes.

b What's this? / What are these?    It's a nose.

c What's this? / What are these?

d What's this? / What are these?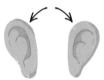

e What's this? / What are these?

1 Look and match.

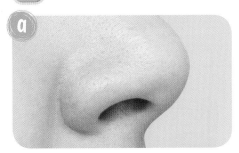

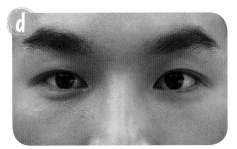

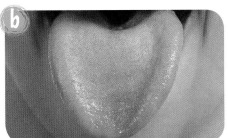

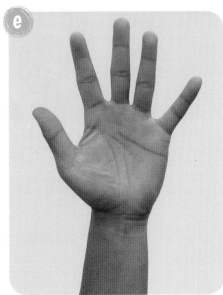

see

hear

smell

touch

taste

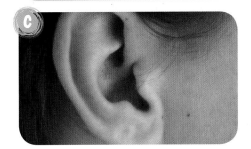

2 Look at the pictures. Look at the letters. Write the words.

a c l s e u m

_ _ _ _ _ _

b i n t j o

_ _ _ _ _

c o b e n s

_ _ _ _ _

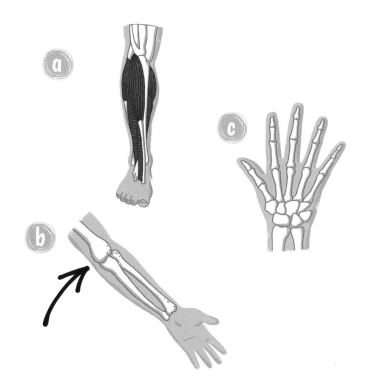

Find the right words

1 **Look and read. Write *yes* or *no*.**

a One girl is eating a healthy snack. _____

b Three children are doing sport. _____

c There is a yellow bin. _____

d A teacher is talking to a girl. _____

2 **Look at the picture in Activity 1 again. Circle the correct option.**

a The ball is *on / next to / under* the slide.

b There are papers *on / in / next to* the floor.

c There is a carton of juice *next to / under / in* the bin.

d One of the girls is sitting *in / on / next to* the bench.

1 🎧 **Listen and tick (✓) the box.**

1 Which snack is healthy?

  ☐  ☐  ☐

2 Which snack is unhealthy?

  ☐  ☐  ☐

3 How many times a day should you eat?

  ☐  ☐  ☐

2 **Correct the words in bold.**

a Brush your **hair** after meals.

_____

b Wash your **head** before you eat.

_____

c Have a **soap** every day.

_____

d Don't watch too much **books**.

_____

e Sleep **five** hours a day.

_____

Find the right words

1 Circle the correct answer.

Is it a jellyfish?

Yes, it is. | No, it isn't.

Is it a bird?

Yes, it is. | No, it isn't.

Is it a fish?

Yes, it is. | No, it isn't.

2 Write the correct answer.

I have got / haven't got a skeleton.

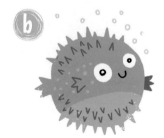

I _____ a skeleton.

1 Write the correct word under each picture.

swim   slither   walk   fly

a

_____

b

_____

c

_____

d

_____

e

_____

f

_____

2 🎧 Listen and colour.

Find the right words

1 Write the correct words.

a It's a / It isn't a beautiful flower.

b It's a / It isn't a tall tree.

c _____ a green leaf.

d _____ a healthy plant.

2 Make sentences about the plant.

a It has got / hasn't got a flower.

b It has got / hasn't got lots of leaves.

c It _____ a thick trunk.

d It _____ a stem.

1 🎧 **Listen and write the numbers.**

a

b

c

2 **Look at the letters. Write the words to complete the sentences.**

a We get tea from _____ .

ochammlie

trsebrriewas

b We get jam from _____ .

c We get chairs from _____ .

seetr

d We get clothes from _____ .

ottnoc

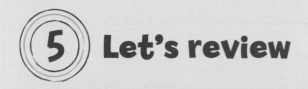

(5) Let's review

Find the right words

1 Look at the photos and circle the correct words.

a *There is / There are* a plant.

b *There is / There are* living things.

c *There is / There are* animals.

d *There is / There isn't* a non-living thing.

2 Look at the picture and read the questions. Write one-word answers.

a What flavour is the jam? _____

b How many sunflowers can you see? _____

c What are the table and chair made from? _____

d What is falling from the unhealthy sunflower? _____

1 Complete the life cycle of animals. Use the words in the box.

reproduce   die   grow   are born

1 _____ ⟶ 2 _____ ⟶ 3 _____ ⟶ 4 _____

2 🎧 Circle the living things green and the non-living things red. Listen and check.

Find the right words

1 Write the words in the correct column.

> share   kind   work hard   clever   listen   honest

I am ...	I ...

2 Look at the pictures and answer the questions.

> working   helping   playing   listening

a What are they doing?
They are _____ .

b What is she doing?
She is _____
her dad.

c Are they _____
together?
Yes, they are.

d Is she _____ to
her parents.
No, she's not.

1 Match the boxes.

a Listen · · your best.

b Respect · · to others.

c Try · · calm.

d Keep · · your family.

2 Choose a word from the box. Write the correct word next to letters a–d.

My name is Chloe. I like school.
I always (**a**)_____
hard and try my best.
Every morning, I make my
(**b**)_____ and get
my (**c**)_____ ready.
I love my parents. I respect and
listen to them.
After school, I like playing in
the (**d**)_____ . I play
fair and always help little ones.

bed

park

schoolbag

work

🎧 **Listen and read.**

Little Franklin and Little Pasteur are at the hospital.

I fell over and broke my arm at my birthday party.

I ate too much and now my tummy hurts.

From now on I'll play carefully.

And I will only eat healthy food.

Surprise!

Yuk! No thanks!

An apple a day ...

keeps the doctor away!

Now act out the story!

Now I know

1 Order the story. Write numbers in the boxes.

2 What happened to Little Franklin? Tick (✓) the correct box.

She broke her …

3 Do you like the story? Colour the apples.

🎧 **Listen and read.**

Little Cuvier is telling his friends about his trip.

Then I went to the Arctic and saw polar bears.

+ = animals

In the rainforest, I saw lots of strange plants.

= plants

My plant is healthy, now.

Plants need water, air and food to live ...

Living things

Plants   Animals

just like animals.

Now act out the story!

1 Order the story. Write numbers in the boxes.

2 Draw and colour a living thing in each place from the story.

3 Do you like the story? Colour the koalas.

🎧 **Listen and read.**

This is a living thing.

The scientists are in the lab. Little Curie is showing her friends the difference between living and non-living things.

Living things need air, water …

and food!

This is a non-living thing. It isn't born and it doesn't reproduce. It doesn't grow or move either.

But it can fall!

Let's be kind.

I'm sorry. Are you ok?

Yes, I'm ok. Next time, I'll take care of the materials!

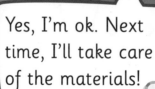

Now act out the story!

1 Order the story. Write numbers in the boxes.

2 In the story, the characters look at a hamster and some rocks. Draw another living and non-living thing you can see in the story.

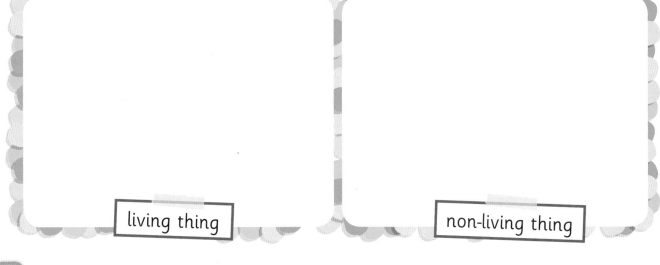

living thing

non-living thing

3 Do you like the story? Colour the test tubes.

Acknowledgements

The authors and publishers acknowledge the following sources of copyright material and are grateful for the permissions granted. While every effort has been made, it has not always been possible to identify the sources of all the material used, or to trace all copyright holders. If any omissions are brought to our notice, we will be happy to include the appropriate acknowledgements on reprinting and in the next update to the digital edition, as applicable.

All the photographs are sourced from Getty Images.

p. 2, p. 65: Cludio Policarpo/EyeEm; p. 5: Dave King/Dorling Kindersley, FrankRamspott/DigitalVision Vectors, LEOcrafts/DigitalVision Vectors, Swillklitch/iStock/Getty Images Plus; p. 5, p. 24: senkoumelnik/iStock/Getty Images Plus, p. 5, p.49, p.63: macrovector/iStock/Getty Images Plus; p. 5, p. 56, p. 57, p. 63: Elvina Kiiamova/iStock/Getty Images Plus; p. 8, p. 13: ourlifelooklikeballoon/iStock/Getty Images Plus; p. 9, p. 97: Yulia-Images/iStock/Getty Images Plus; p. 9: Sebastian Kaulitzki/Science Photo Library, Monsterstock1/iStock/Getty Images Plus, Thomas Barwick/DigitalVision; p. 9, pp. 18–19, p. 47, p. 58, p. 70, p. 71, p. 88: Westend61; p. 10: Lane Oatey/Blue Jean Images, Mike McGinnis/Getty Images Sport, lemonadeserenade/iStock/Getty Images Plus; p. 11, p. 97: LuFeeTheBear/iStock/Getty Images Plus; p. 11: Spauln/E+; p. 11, p. 89: Evan Kafka/The Image Bank; p.11: SerrNovik/iStock/Getty Images Plus, p. 11, p. 68, p. 89: Hero Images; p. 12: Digital Vision, Juice Images/Cultura; p. 13, p. 97: Robert Recker/Corbis; p. 13: PeopleImages/DigitalVision, SPL IMAGES/DigitalVision, Lolkaphoto/iStock/Getty Images Plus, Jose manuel gelpi diaz/Hemera/Getty Images Plus; p. 13, p. 17, p. 79: RusN/iStock/Getty Images Plus; p. 13, p.20: kimberrywood/DigitalVision Vectors; p. 14: BJI/Blue Jean Images, johnwoodcock/DigitalVision Vectors, bortonia/DigitalVision Vectors; p. 15, p. 46, p. 58: Magnilion/DigitalVision Vectors; p. 17: 3sbworld/iStock/Getty Images Plus, DEA/D. DAGLI ORTI/De Agostini; p. 17, p. 79: Jade/Blend Images; p. 17, p. 79: thawats/iStock/Getty Images Plus; p. 17, p. 79: AntonioGuillem/iStock/Getty Images Plus; p. 17, p. 79: bobbieo/E+; p. 20: Okea/iStock/Getty Images Plus, ElsyStudio/iStock/Getty Images plus; p. 20, p. 27, p. 35, p. 61: mocoo/iStock/Getty Images Plus; p. 21, p. 97: Adam Gault/OJO Images; p. 21: Joy Skipper/Photolibrary, Adrian Burke/Photographer's Choice, Jeffrey Coolidge/Stone; p. 22: benoitb/E+, p. 22, p. 29, 81: Cube/Ikon Images; p. 22: Pavlo_K/iStock/Getty Images Plus, Rosemary Calvert/Photographer's Choice, ruzanna/iStock/Getty Images Plus, Caziopeia/E+, davorr/iStock/Getty Images Plus; p. 22, p. 81: Banar Fil Ardhi/EyeEm, Science Photo Library, blueringmedia/E+, mrPliskin/iStock/Getty Images Plus; p. 22, p. 87: scanrail/iStock/Getty Images Plus; p. 22, p. 51, p. 87: Dorling Kindersley; p. 23, p. 97: clubfoto/iStock/Getty Images Plus; p. 23: Kee Wooi Chuah/EyeEm, Brian Macdonald/DigitalVision; p. 23, p. 29: Creative Crop/DigitalVision; p. 23: Roy JAMES Shakespeare/The Image Bank; p. 24: pixelfit/E+, Peter Cade/Iconica, Kajetan Kandler/Taxi, Chris Ryan/Caiaimage; p. 25, p. 29, p. 97: FatCamera/E+; p. 25, p. 64, p. 69, p. 88: KidStock/Blend Images; p. 25: MediaForMedical/UIG, QAI Publishing/Universal Images Group, yuoak/DigitalVision Vectors; p. 26: FatCamera/iStock/Getty Images Plus, Adrian Pope/Photographer's Choice, Image by J. Parsons/Moment, Dudi-artDudi-art/iStock/Getty Images Plus; p. 26, p. 49: Nikiteev_Konstantin/iStock/Getty Images Plus; p. 27: xefstock/E+, ARNICAart/iStock/Getty Images Plus, Sashatigar/iStock/Getty Images Plus, vasabii/iStock/Getty Images Plus; p. 28: energyy/E+, Flashpop/Taxi, Bill Diodato/Stone, Guerilla/Subjects, lee nankervis/Moment, MoMo Productions/Stone, Maria Teijeiro/DigitalVision, mother image/Taxi, Cultura/Charles Gullung; p. 29: Robert Deutschman/The Image Bank, stockce/iStock/Getty Images Plus, Culture Club/Hulton Archive, sunnysideeggs/iStock/Getty Images Plus, Epine_art/iStock/Getty Images Plus, LokFung/DigitalVision Vectors; p. 32: Georgette Douwma/Photographer's Choice, Dave Fleetham/Perspectives, ulimi/DigitalVision Vectors; p. 32, p. 82: Frederic Pacorel/Taxi; p. 33, p. 97: Wild Horizon/Universal Images Group; p. 33: Mint Images/Mint Images RF, JVP photography/Moment, by wildestanimal/Moment; pp. 34–35: Wayne Lynch/All Canada Photos, Steven Kazlowski/Perspectives, DSW Creative Photography/Moment, Jerry Young/Dorling Kindersley; p. 34, p. 83: Sylvain Cordier/Biosphoto, Daniela-Barreto/iStock/Getty Images Plus; p. 35, p. 97: copyright kengoh8888/Moment; p. 35, p. 82: Kristian Bell/Moment; p. 35: Rodrigo Friscione/Image Source, James Hager/robertharding; p. 36: Elisabeth Pollaert Smith/Photographer's Choice RF, Joseph Van Os/The Image Bank, EcoPic/iStock/Getty Images Plus, Yiming Chen/Moment, dpenn/iStock/Getty Images Plus; p. 36, p. 71, p. 98: CraigRJD/iStock/Getty Images Plus; p. 37, p. 97: PhotoAlto/Odilon Dimier/PhotoAlto Agency RF Collections; p. 37: DEA/R. VALTERZA/De Agostini, DEA/C.DANI/De Agostini, Visual China Group, LEMAIRE Stephane/hemis.fr; p. 38: Joe Sohm/Visions of America/Universal Images Group, Marcia Straub/Moment, Fotosearch, John Samu/EyeEm, Peter Cade/The Image Bank, Patricia Hamilton/Moment, morgan stephenson/Moment; p. 38, p. 48: Arterra/Universal Images Group; p. 39: MariaSemj/iStock/Getty Images Plus; p. 40: Dan Porges/Stockbyte, Bigandt_Photography/iStock/Getty Images Plus, Tanya Little/Moment, Reimphoto/iStock/Getty Images Plus; p. 41: Benjamin Van Der Spek/EyeEm, Michael DeFreitas/robertharding, Kim Taylor/Nature

Picture Library, Patricia Doyle/Photographer's Choice, salez/iStock/Getty Images Plus, traveler111/E+; p. 41, p. 83: David Northcott/Corbis Documentary; pp. 42–43: swedewah/E+; p. 44: Ron Bambridge/Caiaimage, DirkRietschel/iStock/Getty Images Plus, Baksiabat/iStock/Getty Images Plus; p. 44, p. 47: AllAGRI/iStock/Getty Images Plus; p. 45: WIN-Initiative/Neleman, DonNichols/E+, Stuart Minzey/Photographer's Choice RF; p. 45, p. 84: Dave King Dorling Kindersley/Dorling Kindersley; p. 45, p. 63, p. 70, p. 98: Tetra Images; p. 46: Johner Images, Diane Macdonald/Moment Open, Photographer Chris Archinet/Moment; p. 46, p. 85: DEA/G. WRIGHT/De Agostini; p. 47: DrPAS/iStock/Getty Images Plus, Image Source, Christian Kunde/EyeEm, Antagain/E+, Antagain/E+; p. 47, p. 49, p. 63: jamtoons/DigitalVision Vectors; p. 48: lzf/iStock/Getty Images Plus, lillisphotography/E+, dhughes9/iStock/Getty Images Plus, Danita Delimont/Gallo Images, Robin James/Cultura, Andrea Edwards/EyeEm, saemilee/DigitalVision Vectors; p. 49, p. 53, p. 98: Australian Scenics/Photolibrary, Geography Photos/UIG/Universal Images Group, Monty Rakusen/Cultura, Photos by R A Kearton/Moment, Luca Aragn/EyeEm; p. 50: antigonigoni/iStock/Getty Images Plus, Ryan Malensek/EyeEm, dszc/E+, Martin Ruegner/Photographer's Choice, Andy Crawford, TongRo Images Inc/TongRo Images, wragg/E+, to_csa/iStock/Getty Images Plus, Del_Mar/iStock/Getty Images Plus; p. 51, p. 98: penguenstok/E+; p. 51: Vicki Vale/FOAP, Kate Davis/Dorling Kindersley, NB_Factory/iStock/Getty Images Plus; p. 53: Lorenzo Vecchia/Dorling Kindersley, József Kardos/EyeEm, Mihai Damian/EyeEm, ppl58/iStock Editorial/Getty Images Plus, Jakob Dupy/EyeEm; p. 56: bgfoto/E+, David Burton/Photolibrary, Bethany Lysaght/EyeEm, Natality/iStock/Getty Images Plus; p. 57, p. 98: Allan Guiang/FOAP, Foap AB/foap, Ana Maria Serrano/EyeEm, Milan Tarlac/EyeEm; p. 58: Justin Sullivan/Getty Images News, atosan/iStock/Getty Images Plus, James D. Morgan/Getty Images News, GK Hart/Vikki Hart/Stockbyte, myshkovsky/iStock/Getty Images Plus; p. 59, p. 98: Robert Alexander/Archive Photos, Colin Gray/Photonica, Atomic Imagery/DigitalVision; p. 59, p. 87: Charles Bowman/Perspectives; p. 60: Monashee Alonso/Caiaimage, Dianne Avery Photography/Moment, David Woolley/DigitalVision, Moncherie/E+, WLADIMIR BULGAR/Science Photo Library, Adam Burton/robertharding; p. 61, p. 98: Kate Jacobs/DigitalVision; p. 61: alvarez/E+, LWA/Dann Tardif/Blend Images; p. 61, p. 98: Siri Stafford/Stone; p. 62, p. 84: DNY59/E+, DNY59/iStock/Getty Images Plus, AVNphotolab/iStock/Getty Images Plus, Valerie Loiseleux/iStock/Getty Images Plus; p. 62, p. 69: carlacdesign/iStock/Getty Images Plus; p. 63: simonkr/iStock/Getty Images Plus, Robert Kneschke/EyeEm, Voysla/iStock/Getty Images Plus, p. 63, p. 87: Lee Pengelly/The Image Bank; p. 64: Walstrom, Susanne, BraunS/E+; p. 65: Henry Arden/Cultura, Richard Boll/Photographer's Choice, Dougal Waters/DigitalVision, Stefano Bianchetti/Corbis Historical, Kevin Button/Moment; p. 65, p. 86, p. 87: Anton Eine/EyeEm; pp. 66–67: Kilian O'Sullivan/Corbis Documentary; p. 68: David Jakle/Image Source, BSIP/Universal Images Group; p. 68, p. 88: Steve Debenport/E+; p. 68, p. 75: JGI/Jamie Grill/Blend Images; p. 68, p. 88: Simon Winnall/Taxi; p. 69, p. 98: Johnnie Davis/DigitalVision, Hill Street Studios/Blend Images, John Anthony Rizzo/UpperCut Images/Getty Images Plus, Asiaselects, Blend Images - KidStock/Brand X Pictures, schiva/iStock/Getty Images Plus; p. 70: Suponev Vladimir/Hemera/Getty Images Plus, J and J Productions/DigitalVision, raigRJD/iStock/Getty Images Plus; p. 71: Voyagerix/iStock/Getty Images Plus, D.Jiang/Moment, p. 71, p. 87: Topic Images Inc./Topic Images; p. 73, p. 98: StHelena/iStock/Getty Images Plus; p. 73: quavondo/E+, bradleym/E+; p. 73, p. 88: RUSS ROHDE/Cultura; p. 75: Andersen Ross/Blend Images, Sam Edwards/Stone; p. 75, p. 98: Ruth Jenkinson/Dorling Kindersley; p. 76: Sonja Dahlgren/Maskot, firina/iStock/Getty Images Plus, Christopher Hope-Fitch/Moment; p. 77: De Agostini Picture Library; p. 78: Rob Lewine/Tetra images, Jose Luis Pelaez Inc/Blend Images, Jill Tindall/Moment, Tomas Rodriguez/Corbis; p. 81: chictype/iStock/Getty Images Plus; p. 82: Ariadne Van Zandbergen/Lonely Planet Images; p. 83: Walstrom/Susanne, Ewen Charlton/Moment, Auscape/Universal Images Group, Antagain/iStock/Getty Images Plus; p. 84: VIDOK/E+, Johner Images/Johner Images Royalty-Free, wepix/E+; p. 85: sytnik/iStock/Getty Images Plus, tiler84/iStock/Getty Images Plus; p. 86: Tom Dobbie/Dorling Kindersley, malcolm park/Photolibrary, DLILLC/Corbis/VCG/Corbis Documentary; p. 87: A. Martin UW Photography/Moment; p. 89: Kerrick/iStock/Getty Images Plus, Yutthana Jantong/EyeEm, artisteer/iStock/Getty Images Plus, Sirikornt/iStock/Getty Images Plus; p. 97: Michael Heim/EyeEm; p. 98: WIN-Initiative/Neleman/WIN-Initiative, Mandy Disher Photography/Moment, shironosov/iStock/Getty Images Plus.

Front cover photography by Dave King/Dorling Kindersley, Kim Taylor/Dorling Kindersley, Mike Hill/Photographer's Choice, artpartner-images/Photographer's Choice, Jerry Young/Dorling Kindersley, cynoclub/iStock/Getty Images Plus, Tim Flach/Stone, TS Photography/Photographer's Choice, Kei Uesugi/Stone, Jackie Edward/ImageZoo, MarkBridger/Moment, Paul Marcellini/Nature Picture Library, Chase Dekker Wild-Life Images/Moment, stillifephotographer/Stone, stilllifephotographer/Stone, Nicholas Eveleigh/DigitalVision.

Designer: emc design

The authors and publishers would like to thank the following illustrators:

Michael Buxton (Advocate Art) pp5 (1, 2 and 3), 8, 16, 32 (eel), 34 (fish), 36, 38, 39, 40, 44, 46, 48, 52, 56 (sunflowers), 58 (gorilla), 60, 62, 64, 70, 72, 74, 76, 77, 78, 79, 80, 81, 82, 83, 86; Gaby Zermeño pp4, 6–7, 9, 11, 13 (character), 17 (character), 18–19, 21, 23, 25 (character), 29 (character), 30–31, 33, 35 (characters), 37, 41, 42, 45 (character), 47 (character), 49 (character), 51 (character), 53, 54–55, 57 (character), 59 (character), 61 (character), 63 (character), 65, 66–67, 69 (character), 71, 73, 75, 77 (character), 90, 91, 92, 93, 94, 95.

Unit 1

  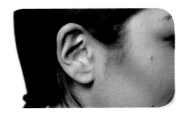

Unit 2

Unit 3

Unit 4

Unit 5

Unit 6